CW00541704

REARRANGING THE SKY

Also by Frances Wilson

Where the light gets in
(Poet & Printer, 1992)

Close to Home
(Rockingham Press, 1993)

Frances Wilson

Rearranging
the Sky

For Leah —
with all good wishes —
and love and thanks
for your continuous
support
    Frances
        October 2004

Rockingham Press

Published in 2004 by
The Rockingham Press
11 Musley Lane,
Ware, Herts SG12 7EN
www.rockinghampress.com

British Library Cataloguing-in-Publication Data

A catalogue record for this book
is available from the British Library

ISBN 1 873468 98 9

Printed in Great Britain
by Biddles Limited
King's Lynn, Norfolk

In memory of
Harry Wilson

Acknowledgements

Acknowledgements are due to the editors of the following in which some of these poems first appeared: *London Magazine, The Rialto, Smiths Knoll, Acumen, Other Poetry, North, Staple, Seam, Soundings, Prop, Smoke* and several anthologies.

'Thread' won first prize in the Lake Aske Competition 1995; 'The Musician's House' won second prize in the Manchester Open Poetry Competition 1997; 'Not Darcy Bussell' won first prize in the Pittshanger Open Poetry Competition 2000; and 'Fairytale Ending' was commended in the Bridport Poetry Competition 2003.

Three of these poems appeared in the pamphlet collection *Where the light gets in*, published by Poet & Printer in 1992.

Cover design by Frances Wilson.

Contents

Touching up the Bloodstains

Years after he'd moved out,
moved in with his girl-friend,
she still couldn't face up
to repainting his bedroom.

When they'd first stripped it,
awaiting the baby, they'd unpeeled
the whole history of the house
in layers of paper, right back

to Victorian roses. It had felt
like walking on graves, disturbing
more than a hint of fingers
left on the brickwork.

Finally she had to accept it –
eight years of adolescent male
graffiti to be whitewashed. It took over
a week, including the reading.

But she refused to do up
the bathroom, the burn on the sill
worn faint as a thumb-print
where he'd rested a cigarette

while mending the cistern,
that first weekend they left him
alone, and he'd painted his bedroom
ceiling black, with bloodstains.

Living Next Door to a Topiarist

She saw him from her kitchen window,
shears slack in his grip, eyeing the bushes
as she gulped coffee, unstacked last night's dishes,
programmed the washing. Then she forgot him,
flinging a last angry warning upstairs,
backing the car out, gravel exploding.

When she rushed home that evening just in time
to haul out the lounger and grab a last wedge
of sunshine, his box was ship-shape, the bay
a green flame; and he was still standing
rhythmically cutting up twigs into fragments
over the compost, snip-snip, snip-snip,
ticking the seconds away, the whole day
she thought, suddenly snapping,
"You could borrow our shredder,"
adding, "it would save hours."

Between them the air was aromatic
with cut grass, last pinks, crushed bay
leaves. All round them the smoky dust
of evening settled on laurel and privet,
geraniums burned in the dusk by the shed.

"What for?" he said.

Thread

In a walled garden with a bench which was once on a station,
(the platform's now buried in nettles; only a drop in a footpath,
like missing a heart-beat, betrays it)

where, freckled in shade, two women sit
risking the precarious balance of language,
trusting the net of their friendship,

while old and whiskerless, a blind cat
bumps between wall and shrub to a well of steps, follows his howl
to his bowl and a box by a door where his deaf twin is sleeping,

a grub
small as the half-moon on a child's little finger-nail,
inches his way down a thread he's unwinding from within
his own body –

twists

and, for a second, a current of sunlight
becomes a crack in the air, opening.

Breathless

Even running late, I can't not glance back
at the magnolia behind the library
which reaches almost to the roof
where once you could see the loudspeaker
which went on blaring out the all-clear
years after the war was over, to call
the firemen; and I wonder every time
what happened to that plucky young woman,
the midwife who lived there, who was up
at our house in three minutes flat,
naked and wet under her coat from the bath
she'd leapt out of when I rang in terror
because my baby, who is now thirty-six,
was blue and not breathing.

Boy on a Bicycle

You'd not recognise
that sullen lad
who slouches at the back
of your classes,
how he holds himself now

erect as a heron,
intent on this rod
he'd kiss willingly.
It is bigger than he is,
his passion he balances

navigating his bike
one-handed in the slip-stream
of traffic, till,
with a flick of his wrist
he reels himself in

towards the towpath
where his heart is,
a few muddy feet of brink
whose depth he fathoms
better than physics.

All week he has been lying
low, thinking himself here
in this hollow he's made
his and hallowed
with bread and maggots.

Now, snug in his sludge-
coloured anorak, in the murk
of reed and meadowsweet,
nothing ruffles him
but the wind.

17

My Mother with one Green Earring

Something someone says – and out of the blue I'm back
with sun on a red pub carpet: that birthday we took
my mother out for lunch (before her will broke,
bits flying everywhere, all of us cut); her look
of shocked admiration for my punk son beside her
in studs and chains, for my glossy, lacquered daughter;
their affection for her gaucheness, her coy ordering of cider,
her awe at the glitz of this place where we'd brought her –
the soft blood-beat of muzak, the smokescreens, the alcohol,
(and her church right opposite); how a stray piece of cress
got caught in her hair, in sunlight, as she bent to her cole-
slaw; the three of us riveted, wordless, the hard-won excess
of their outfits eclipsed by the effortless dangling
of my mother's one glittering, filigree, emerald earring.

Thrush, Peartree, You

The first thing you show us is the thrush
through a kitchen window so spick and span
it might be wide open. Its plain frame
offers a picture of a peartree, perfectly
composed, as if everything were easy,
as if even friendship needed no effort
to flourish. Bees are at work elsewhere. Flowers
open while we're not looking. Even your stroke
is told as a joke – that time you went missing,
how you send things flying – made light of.

The only dark is the barn, a backdrop
to all that froth of blossom. The tree
is bent double, knobbled and chopped off,
like an awkward gesture love has made lovely.
In the crook of its fork a mistle-thrush sits
tight; her nest, breast- and egg-shaped, fits
snug as a fist. Her eye, watching us watching,
is a knot-hole in wood through which everything
will happen. She's a time-bomb. If you stopped
breathing, you'd think you would hear her tick.

Abroad

Even by the outskirts of Calais it's like being let loose
in a sweet shop – all those old favourites I'd forgotten
the taste of: *Rappel! Prix des carburants.* I roll them round
on my tongue, gob-stoppers of sounds I can't get enough of:
Virages sur dix kilometres. Aire du champs du drap d'or.
They melt on my breath into more than recognition.
This is reclamation, primitive as pronouns, possessives.

But I keep it to myself, mouth them out of the window
under the Butterworth adagio you're tuned to, remembering
your mother's endless reciting of every road sign:
Give way. Reduce speed now. She'd haul in each word
like a life-line. With amazement which was not quite delight
(her hold wasn't sure enough) she'd arrive at comprehension.
It drove us all mad. But she wasn't. She was abroad,

trying to recover through the flavour of words the meaning
of a country she dimly remembered she'd once belonged in.

The Musician's House

This year we're too late for the cherries.
Unpicked, they're dropping. Rumour has it
a wild boar, rooting among them at dawn,
was spotted by the shepherd, who today
is strimming the meadow, his monstrous wasp-
noise leaving a scent of mint which thickens
quickly to rotting. His daughters bring us
armfuls of lavender and hover like moths,
then show us chanterelles they've picked
with their grandmother. Her cat is pregnant.

I cook and clean needlessly, playing peasant
with a broom I could have made, but the bush
is still blooming. The musician's terrace
is littered with husks of chestnut catkins,
small snake skins. I've been there. I've seen
his new steps, the workman's rubble topped
with gloves, fat as if hands were left in them;
ants printing out and in under the lintel
their indecipherable messages. His greengages
are perfect, little firm buttocks, but bitter.

And I am aimless, convalescent, want something
but it's not the musician although he's expected.
People swear they've heard him, seen lights. Not me,
though last night, late, we passed a stranger
who greeted us, and someone has picked his one lemon.
From where I'm sitting, if I leaned, I could see
his windows, only I'm preoccupied with a lapful
of shrivelled berries, sweet as raisins, but dusty
with mildew which dries my throat as I spit out stones
down the hillside: last year, this year, sometime

Thinking of Swans

reminds me of a woman I knew who married this man
because once on a journey together his car headlights
picked out a dead swan hanging from an overhead cable

and he shinned up, then plucked it and roasted it
on a campfire by the roadside. Far better, she said,
than what happened to Leda. But she too was deceived.

She didn't live happily though he wasn't unfaithful
exactly. And I've always been dubious about that
myth of monogamy. Swans. They're not what they seem.

There's something about that black mask and the way
they fold their wings before laying their necks along
their backs which reminds me of a conjuror's hands

fanned to show they're empty. You can't trust them.
That summer after our friends' house was ransacked
I lay awake night after night trying not to think

of torchlight fingering everything, and black gloves
like white gloves wrong-side out, printlessly ripping
everywhere open, the whole house adrift with swansdown.

The Last Thing

The last thing he needed
was the wrong phone-call,
the wrong voice, any number
divisible by two, mornings
trying to match up his socks.

The last thing he needed
was a cheery word, a good
book, a slap on the back,
a new hobby; being reminded
of other people's suffering.

He could do without
small girls in flip-flops
jigging round daddies, couples
shopping together, evenings
smelling of charcoal and travel.

He needed the last thing
he had wanted – her, her hair;
lifting her hair; her mouth,
her soft rasping voice saying
the things she used to say before

she said those last things.

Under the Skin

I am searching to find a poem
for my sister, the one I used to play with,
got ticked off for talking in the dark with;

the sister who hauled me after her
onto the garage roof to drop down
pine-needles from the guttering.

And now it's those pine-needles
which are distracting me.
I can feel their pricking softness.

I know how the wind blew them
into drifts along the border edges,
how they got into socks and carpets,

that smell when we threw them on the fire,
how they spat and sparked upwards.
Which brings me to the chimney pot

which is now in my garden, and the sister
who dodged bull-dozers and charmed
builders when the house was demolished

fifty years later, to rescue two
chimneys so we could both hold
on to a piece of our childhood.

Double Summer Time

The evening my mother washed my hair
and it was too hot for a gas fire,
too late to let me blow it dry outside,
too risky with my history of rheumatism
to send me to bed with it seeping
into the pillow, my brain rusting,

she pushed up the bathroom window
and sat me with my back to the garden
beyond which, each afternoon, prisoners
of war gathered waiting for transport;
young men, smoking, scuffing up gravel,
their voices guttural, unintelligible.

Our tea was timed so they'd be gone
when my sisters were allowed out again
on those long double summer time evenings,
while I was sent up to bed to be kept awake
by daylight and listening to them playing.
So it must have been my sisters

who whistled at my hair, permanently waved
from plaiting, rippling to the sill.
I thought it was a soldier who'd fallen
for me, but I mustn't look round or the sash
might snap or I'd slip or something
worse, to do with the war, would happen.

No Love Lost

But there must have been a lot of love
lost between their meeting on a train
out of London and their last parting.

I picture the aunt we knew, plump,
moustached – but always, my mother said
wistfully, a honey-pot, irresistible –

in a blue feather hat and sporting
her fox fur (though later she'd hurl bricks
at the hunt which crossed her farmland)

seated opposite this gingery man,
lean and clean-shaven but threadbare,
going nowhere, who'd lost everything;

how she spied the cyrillic of his book
as he bowed impeccably to retrieve
something she'd let fall, rummaging.

From that moment on she took over
his halting conversation, his future,
harnessing his statelessness,

his desire, his muscle, to the market
garden she had set her heart on.
She'd speak for him, pay for him,

they'd work shoulder to shoulder
without ever touching
though they gave off a heat

even twenty years later
when they separated, salvaging
and splitting what they could

of her capital; hopes unrecoverable;
no longer speaking and now clearly
with no love lost between them.

The Colour of the Man

Think earths: burnt umber, terra rosa, brown madder alizarin.
Think peat water, fires, torn letters curling;
beech, crisp and coppered; frost, ground beaten, ringing.

Think feathers, Rhode Island and pheasant. Trip wire, traps,
snapped twigs, blood drying.

Think rust grey hair, flattened by damp, smelling of petrol;
small white teeth, sharp canines, slav cheekbones,
face angled towards the nose, a muzzle.

Then think gentle, voice soft, that labial language.
Quick smile, like a dog's, thirsty. Dog-fox, wary,
loping off into the spinney, the earth she'd given him.

A refugee. Homeless.

True gentleman who kissed her
once only, the night their house burned down,
on her forehead, like a mother.

Letting Off Steam

She'd stand there, bunched
and breathless in some sweater
she'd knitted without a pattern,
pumping water from the well,
left, right, left, right,
like a windscreen wiper
on speed or a sergeant-major,
fuming at the drop
in the price of pigs, the rise
in the cost of chicken feed,
at the stacked trays of eggs
to be washed and held up
to the candle; and daily
his disappearance to the wood
with his gun to his precious
pheasants, without a word
to her, why even his cousin
who'd visited, the one who
embroidered the cushion covers
in the sitting room, such
a nice woman and not a word
of English, you could tell
even she had been shocked –
ninety-eight, ninety-nine,
one hundred, the pressure
rising and rising and rising

Fairy Tale Ending

Not in a castle or a wood, you'll find him by water.
Follow the towpath, over one bridge and another
past millpond and cut. Ignore the warnings of geese,
the blind donkey braying. Don't be side-tracked
by words carved in bark of poplars nor the shape
of their leaves. You'll find him past the weir –
woodcutter, guardian of sluice-gates, carp and grayling,
the coots' nest beached against the bridge's buttress.

Not what you'd wish for in a damsel in distress,
this belligerent old lady in a blue straw hat
she'd burnt under the grill while drying it;
who fell head over heels on the pavement
outside the greengrocer's as the woodcutter
was passing. She can't have been easy
to pick up, with her cardigans, and onions
rolling under his feet and making for the gutter.

He might have wished for someone prettier.
But she was charmed to be taken home
in his battered van like the one she had
driven for years without a licence or scratch
with no-one the wiser or the worse for it.
And by the time he left her, hours later –
unharmed, nerves soothed, the tea so neat
on the tray you'd think a maid had laid it –

she had a list which lasted seven years
of quests for him to perform to earn her
undying love and a few pounds each weekend.
Rewiring, pruning, there was nothing he'd not do
for her – he even made peace with a neighbouring
old lady she'd thumped over the communal garden.
And she'd brook no criticism of his leaving
his first wife, nor his remarrying.

It was he who kept the key to her door,
who was sent for to open up that morning,
to find her sitting in the kitchen where death
had dropped by as she was getting the milk out.
And he stood at the crematorium, twisting
and twisting his fingers, a balding prince
with a young wife and a retinue of children,
still handsome, saying over and over:
What shall I do now with Saturday mornings?

My Aunt's Sow

Unsurprising, once you'd thought of it,
her adoration of Gloria. It was mutual.
Mirrors to whiskery glorification of flesh
they both wallowed in. A sisterhood.

Gloria, caricature conspirator, huge ears
flapping for messages to be scratched
in code on that soft spot at the back
of them. That look – ecstatic or concealing

a joke. Watchful, secretive eyes,
their blond lashes an unfinished make-over.
Her snout mobile, as if satellite
tracking. How asleep, she played dead.

Sisterhood. Conspiracy. Surrogacy.
Litter after litter with invariably a runt
my aunt showed me how she bottle-fed. Nameless.
All except Gloria, who'd never be for the chop.

Storm

While others had sheds lifted and dropped
on greenhouses, chimneys toppled,
she had her neighbour's shirt, muddied,
bundled underneath the flowering currant.

Washed, it still smelled unfamiliar
as she nosed her iron into its armpits,
buttoned it up, straightened the collar,
laid it on his doorstep, beside the milkbottle.

Using my Neighbour's Hose

I honestly hadn't noticed
what was missing till the evening
I was watering the perpetual spinach,
when a bramble latched onto my ankle
and it all seemed suddenly a chore,
unaccountably lonely

and I registered he'd mended it
and how much I had liked
watching that fine line of silver
shoot up at odd angles,
dodging the wet up my legs
if I didn't position the hose carefully
so the leak would seep underneath

or throw out visible fuse-wire to grapple
a leaf; how, as I hauled in the heavy
coils to their wheel by his greenhouse
I'd still see the rainbow spray
insisting on escaping, though I'd turned
off the water – irrepressible as the delight
I'd not even noticed I was feeling.

High Spot

It was the horsemen appearing
afterwards, slowly
over the brow of the hill, like rocks
forced up by some seismic contraction,
or gods whose portent was the eclipse
we'd just witnessed.

We clustered round them, acolytes,
hands hovering towards their horses' rumps
as if the gloss might rub off on us
while they recounted how they'd timed their ride
to reach the crossing at the valley bottom
precisely as it happened,
how they'd reined in the horses
to stop them drinking
while they leaned to watch
the sun's disappearance in the puddle.

Then, at a twist of a wrist
they were off, swaying away from us,
their delicate, soft-thudding placement
of each crescent hoof on turf and tarmac
leaving no imprint under the trees
where those uniform half-moons of light
we'd marvelled at had so recently fallen.

On the Screen

If you look carefully you can see the sea. There.
Just a line. You should have seen the shadow
of that gate before the sun went in, as blue
as molten metal. And that's an orchid, only common purple
but a shame it's blurred. Odd how half closed eyes
can give a kind of definition, while the unfocused lens
loses the point. A pity photographs are never right.

I took this shot to try to catch the lark. When I arrived,
you'll not believe it, but those sheep were on their knees,
cropping the grass, of course, but it was weird, that
and a prize wind pummelling the hedgerow, and the way
the sun went in and out, evasive, and the trees
all leaning east, as if they too knew something.

I'm not sure what that is. Could be my hair
blowing across, or just the light got in. And yet
I swear I took it hoping something would show up.
You see, it was the song I wanted, on and on,
cardiographic zig-zag peaks of sound, monitoring
the dawn. The state of the earth's heart.
It made you hold your breath in case it stopped.

Ex

He has dressed in his best
shirt for her, as if
she were his true love –
which she is, the first ever,
despite his wife, the others.

He longs to keep touching
her hair where it feathers
her ears, her intricate knees,
her small fingers spread
on the ball he has bought her.

He'd like to hold her
all the time. But she's off,
sure of her precarious feet,
after pigeons'
last minute evasions

and the ball
he now bounces and bounces,
the slap-slap of his hand
and the ground a rhythm
to call her back to him.

Almost he wants her to fall
so she'll staunch
with her wails the ache
he feels these hours
when she's his,

when her shadow growing
longer is a movement
nearer leaving her
at the door; seeing his ex-
wife's face slammed shut.

Not Darcy Bussell

Not Darcy Bussell, but with a name equally improbable,
only this house could have bred or invented her – a house full

of dormers and alcoves and the patter of leaves receding
into the hush of long afternoons; a house so overshadowed

by lime trees it seemed under water, imperfectly remembered;
only a house with wings, boarded up, unused now, could harbour

this diminutive woman with her capering and gestures and frizz
of rust-coloured hair as if a stray ray of sunlight, squeezed

in and refracted from a bevel of mirror, had not quite set it aflame,
merely singed it; tiny woman with her supple girl's body and hands

like a squirrel monkey's (which unaccountably move you to tears)
and her trills of delight or command like gusts through wind chimes

for the pupils she lined up and loved, perfect toys, compliant
but alive, who pirouetted to the musical-box tunes plinked out

on the piano by her plump mother with the fey smile at each plié,
or some dream of stardom; always in shadow, trees playing

their different lime light, moonshine. And beyond all this,
beyond the old horse pensioned off in the shade, the swish-swish

of his tail rhythmic as soft soles on chalked floorboards, the last
stop on a branch line, its platform mid-Saturday, mid-August

empty; smell of cow parsley, oil on sleepers, sweet wrappers, tar;
bright tracks wavering away towards London, or somewhere.

Figs

Consider this fig tree beside the water tank.
It is an awning spread to make shade for us.
Duck under – and there, like a child's dream
of conkers, are figs. New laid. Everywhere.

A self-replenishing sweet-hoard to gorge on.
You can fill a scooped skirt with their perfections.
And it feels like thrift, not greed, stocking up
against famine. A race memory of discovering honey.

All day, even in fiercest heat, under this tree
is a sanctuary. Figs drop like sudden insights
while above a thousand flat green hands are fanned
and overlapping, each leaf as big as a bikini.

No wonder Adam and Eve wore them. But why
we picked the apple is beyond me – you'd think figs
would do better for An Introduction To Sex, the way
they hang, soft skin sacks, plump or wrinkled.

Which reminds me of the dogs we pass on our way
to the boulangerie, who turn tail and swagger off,
doggy rear-views askew, displaying their small figs,
oblivious of the heat, no doubt after some bitch.

Getting a taste for it

How could I have known
with no television and the Odeon
a bus-ride away, past the common
I was forbidden?

And what could I have learned
from my mother's lips
brushing my forehead
shy mother who went to such pains
to explain menstruation
how could I feel ignorant?

Or my grandparents, role-models
for a couple – she, always cold,
who would barter a butterfly flutter
on my cheek for warm breath
in the small of her back?
He, deflecting caresses with books?

No wonder it came as a shock.
Such dry and tentative touchings
couldn't possibly have prepared me
for what seemed like being eaten.

It must be a mistake.
Nobody had taught him
you don't put a spoon you've licked
back in the jam-pot.

I'd just have to meet him again,
just once, just to tell him
and to ask him – who else? –
what to do with my nose
which had seemed so enormous?
and if he *honestly* enjoyed it,
like stilton, or wine?

Getting off at Pisa

Long before Erica Jong I'd begun
to unzip it, on a packed train
from Genoa. Pure luck we picked
that carriage so I had to push
past this soldier to find one free
seat to dump our baggage, leaving
me in the corridor, my back
to the partition beyond which
my friend nursed our two
rucksacks and disowned me.

Like slipping off a dress (the shift
was in fashion) I shrugged off
public approval. All I wanted
was his mouth. This was pre-sixties
when kissing was an end in itself,
delicious as licking off icing
from a cake and having it, non-stop
while the train rocked through
peerless Ligurian countryside.

There was nothing between us –
no promises, not a postcard –
no language except tongues – yet I'm left
with a flavour of something unsullied
like the memory of a perfect picnic –
and though shameless, not dangerous.
He may have been going all the way
to Rome, but I was getting off at Pisa.

Sunstroke

It wasn't jealousy, that Saturday, made me faint.
It was the sun, honestly, and watching the vet
give the pigs injections. There's nothing desirable
about fainting – a hiss expanding and your skull
contracting. Coming round after bashing your temple
on a pig trough is no laugh either. And I bet a limp
twelve-year-old hoisted by that vet down the track
didn't look glamorous like those pale-faced heroines
do, bones broken, jolted to safety on the backs
of wagons. But more than the strength of his arms
containing me, what I felt was magnetism
drawing together the vet and you, my big sister,
over my head, but carrying me along, accidentally,
by some stroke of the sun and the pigs' witchery.

Missing Elvis

First time round I missed out
on Elvis – too whirled off my feet
by my own circular skirt to notice,
by how my new pony-tail flicked and hung.

So I ducked the shock of Rock
and Roll. I was turned on enough
just by wearing stilettos, how walking
was down to my hips, the way they swung.

I must have heard Heartbreak Hotel
sobbed above the hubbub of pubs, words
pumped out through velvet. I picked up
the beat, but missed the implications,

far too carried away by kissing
itself to go further; applying my sugar-
pink candyfloss lipstick to be licked off;
the exploration of mouths, teeth, tongues.

Decades later, living through
a different fifties, now kisses mean more
or less than themselves, I'm glad
not to miss him, this second time round,

as my twenty-year-old daughter
and her boyfriend stick up his picture, sleep
together beneath his surprisingly familiar
lop-sided brooding; imitate that sound,

his cowslick, while I ransack Oxfam
for signed photos to send them, records
I wish I'd possessed; only now feel
his coarse beauty's oddly innocent appeal.

Pigeon Fancier

"It's easier as a grandfather," he said.
He looked a good man, broad like his vowels,
awkward at being filmed, not just from shyness
but because photographs and things are women's stuff.

His glance slipped from the camera as if his words
had gone off course. "Your own, you treat 'em tough."
A shrug. "It's a hard world." Something didn't fit.

All the while he talked
his blunt fingers stroked the soft round breast
and fanned the docile wings.

And I wondered how his children used to feel, watching,
still stinging from the rough edge of his tongue.
No wonder they dawdled, didn't come straight home.

Covering Her Tracks

Days when she paced to the limits of the house, caught
herself pausing at the stir of a curtain, vibrations of water,
not knowing what she almost thought or what she was after,

she'd carry her coffee round with her. Then, as if marking a plot
she'd leave half empty cups in places she instantly forgot,
wanting a fresh sensation on her tongue, liking it hot.

He'd stumble across them, gone cold, complain as he bent
to retrieve them, wondering what her restlessness meant,
unsettled by such signs of discontent.

And she knew. So if she went out, like unspringing a trap
she'd first recover her tracks, search out each tell-tale cup
from whatever concealed corner, then meticulously wash up;

because, if she were killed or suddenly died elsewhere,
those half drunk cups of coffee, as if she were still there
would be one thing he'd not have to bear.

Amanuensis

Driving to the hospital, now she knows
he's pulled through, she permits herself
to think the unthinkable, can admit
she's quite liked, these hot nights
sleeping untouched, spread-eagled.

It even feels holistic to allow
herself now some make-believe
grieving; to wonder which jumper
she'd have chosen never to wash, assuming
his mantle, his tastes in music.

She smiles at the thought of their friends'
shock, not recognising his amiable
inventive invectives in her mouth,
wondering what on earth has got into her.
But like lifting the edge of a scab

she can't stop now. How did she miss
noticing that tree she's passed daily
for a week could be one of his etchings?
In her mind she blocks in its masses
and like finding a name for a pain

she knows she'd start painting
as he did. She can picture his studio,
dust thickening on his bric-a-brac
and herself in his shirtsleeves completing
a canvas she can't wait to show him.

Wool over my eyes

When I think of the beginning, it's Rosy
Catchpole I remember, knitting everywhere:
in the playground, round the coke stove
in winter. Rib. Cable. Moss. She could pass
slipped stitches over whole jumpers
while we were still unpicking dishcloths.

A round-shouldered old woman at ten,
with eyebrows which sloped like a circumflex
in perpetual perplexity at everything,
she didn't care if she failed the 11+
the Grammar was a bus-ride too far for her.
I can see her, agog while I bragged

about going to boarding school, lording it
with stories of midnight feasts swallowed
from my sister, who was full of it.
Rosy Catchpole. The sudden cessation
of the click, click, ominous as a clock
stopping. Her shocked: "Oh! I couldn't.

I'd miss my Mum." And the penny dropping.

Going Back

Never have a dog, especially not one of those grizzled, rough-
haired, sturdy, always game terriers with overhanging tufts

of eyebrows which swivel as his eyes follow your every movement
while you check what to take back from rooms which look different

even before you pack; which he picks up along with his ball
which he drops on top of your pile of folded uniform, all

with name-tapes in italics which you chose and are dying to swank
about until you think where you'll not be when you unpack the trunk

your dog went frenzied at the sight of, paroxysms of sniffing as if
he'd been stung, but now he's subsided, chin on paws, has quit

pretending it's a walk, and his stump of a tail barely moves
as you stroke him too often in passing, wishing you could shove

him inside your pyjama-case to be with you at night, to cuddle
instead of your teddy who hasn't his smell of old puddles.

And suddenly you can't bear it, his quivering, that pathetic
'Please pity me' look – why should you, he's all right jack,

soon all your corners of the house will be his – so you kick
him, as your mother comes in with your freshly pressed tunic

and cries, "Oh, poor little Nick, you know how he hates you going!"
Then she stumbles over him too, just not looking what she's doing.

Earning my Stripe

My first dance dress
was midnight blue taffeta
but too big for me.

Its milky sheen cool-fingered
as if by accident my body
moving separately inside it.

Two days later, his letter
on the shelf in the alcove
off the hall where we'd danced.

News of it reached me,
the postmark spotted
and passed on, long before

I'd not recognised my name
in his writing. It beat
a distinction or an interview

for Oxford. But he slipped up
the next Saturday, smouldering
through the Main Gates

with a selection
of the First Eleven, come
to take me for a ride.

It wasn't the dress, the dance,
not even the letter, let alone
"Love, Gareth" that I wanted –

it was only the envelope
in my left breast blazer
pocket, its stripe of white

utterly different
from the one I'd always had
for good deportment.

Heat Wave

An evening after weeks of evenings so sultry
they'd at last let us out between supper and bedtime;
dampness coming up from the grass on the meadow
where they left it uncut longest, between the pet-shed

and the lacrosse pitch; not twilight but almost,
the grounds contracting to our voices and the hot scent
of elder and cedar coming on strong and foreign;
all that, and the impact of plimsoles on spongy turf,

the precise ratio of my weight to the height of backs
bent over to ankles, knees, almost to upright –
I was india rubber. I could have jumped beyond bounds.
Home. Anywhere. But here was all I wanted: Denise,

luminous in white aertex, steadying herself; her gasp
then her shout: "Gosh, aren't you wizard at leap-frog!"

My Sister as a Landgirl

You're the one standing sidelong
one foot on the runner of the tractor
you're all leaning against. You're looking
straight at the camera, red lipstick black
in black and white. I'd like to call you
brazen but I think you're just daring
anyone to question if you're tough enough.

Maybe you dropped it once, a chance remark
one teatime, "I want to be a landgirl!" – fed up
with school and old enough to understand
there was more to war than playing shadows
on the cellar ceiling during air-raids. Maybe
I saw the picture in some wartime station
waiting-room, gave you the same home perm.

Because you say there couldn't be a photo,
it's impossible, you were only fourteen
when war ended. But when I think of you now,
out walking your chilly hillsides, I see those
dungarees clearly. You'd be surprised,
my stalwart sister, at all the outfits I hook over
your shoulders. How good you look.

Aunt's Advice

Find something stable, an upturned crate
to sit on in a shed smelling of bedstraw
and sweet cicely. Don't forget, a goat will eat
anything, even your hair when your head's down
wedged in that miraculous triangular cavity
between her haunch and belly.

Latch onto her udder, that two-fingered
fat pouch you are coaxing milk from
like emptying bagpipes left out in a downpour.
And remember she's a prankster, a dancer
on tables. If for a second you waver
from watchfulness – lulled, as you are,
by the steady rubbery drumming –
she'll pick it up, put the hoof in.

But it's only innocent devilry in spite
of those cloven toes. She wants you
to notice her, nudging the bumps
of her horns into the crook of your arm,
smelling salty and sweet, a cream-
cheesy scent, like a baby's sweat.

Convalescent

Because he's ill, the house is muffled.
I've stuffed the telephone
under cushions. It still rings
but muted. We are not quite cut off.

The postman knows better than to knock.
He slips in letters like asides.
I turn away callers. Conversation is costly.
We bank up our energy for our own uses.

From a flickering picture-box, stories
of wars reach but don't touch us.
The truth is here where we live
within a moat of quiet, under a siege

of our choosing. And we are not unhappy
in this life stripped to fresh sheets
and his chair downstairs, our hoards
of forty years of books and music.

This is how things used to be
when our children were ill – cushions
piled on made-shift beds I could watch
through the hatch, bringing syrups, singing,

the house contracting to lamplight, sounds
from outside arriving as if through water –
as if I could take my world back into myself,
further back, safer even than in a cradle.

From this Window

This is the window you watch from
when I drive off without you.
I used to believe I was angry
when you checked how I backed
out into the flow of traffic.

But now I know I like it – your
face at the window, how you pretend
to be dead-heading houseplants,
that look, instantly masked by a silly
grimace to hide your real feelings.

It's here your mother would lift up
our baby daughter, would beguile her
with swallows and chimneys,
holding her soft-stemmed hand
to teach her to wave us good-bye.

Widow

He used to say it was his favourite
Christmas present. He dined out
for months on how he'd not get another one
till he'd used it: the gravestone
I bribed two dustmen to rescue
from the dump and lug up our side-way
that winter they tidied the churchyard.

He planned to lay it or to build
a feature or a folly but didn't
get round to it. So it just stayed
leaning easily under the elder,
snail-trails and shadows crossing
its surface like memory; sunbursts
of lichen showing our air was healthy.

With its worn curlicues like arms
akimbo, it felt like a friend
waiting so we could peg out
our washing together. Elizabeth.
I never knew if she was 'beloved'
or 'faithful' or even who she was
married to, and now 'wife of'
is getting less and less certain.

Homeopathy

Months after, in his studio,
she found his beard-clippings
in an ashtray with curls
of pencil sharpenings

and at the back of a drawer
an ounce of St Bruno Flake
with his pipes from twenty years
before, when he'd stopped smoking.

She imagined grinding them down
to pigment, to a fine powder,
to inhale, to swallow at meal-times,
during the night, whenever it hurt,

if she wanted to be cured.

Eating Out

Most things I can manage alone now:
sleeping, walking, driving, even this break
away: kettle-holes, drumlins. The sunsets.

But a visit to this restaurant recommended
in the brochure which we'd have treated
ourselves to the evening before leaving,

for this I'll have to find some fancy
dress, put my face on, mascara and lipstick
now a foreign language, to order the right wine

to go with the cous-cous au poulet,
the coulis de framboise a circlet
of blood round my apricot sorbet –

not allowing myself to have at the table
beside me that novel I can't put down
or a crossword, to come between us.

The World, the Universe, Space

I drove north for Christmas.
Passing the cemetery, it hurt
to think of the tree we'd planted
for you, out in the cold

and leafless. Then I remembered
your ashes were snug
in the plastic urn
inside the cardboard box

near the radiator
in your studio
beside the view you loved
over the garden

on top of the speaker
where you used to keep
that plaster mask I hate
which I've put on the floor

under the table, like the skull
in Holbein's painting
of The Ambassadors, placed there
to hold the picture in balance.

Just Listen

The way you'd turn
to Radio 3, listen, then ask:
"So, who wrote this?"
It could have been your way
to show me up or to show off,
except I knew you
didn't have a scrap
of brag or malice;
and I began to notice
your tone of voice,
how you were trying
to show me how to listen
with my ears, my skin,
until I began to understand
how much you wanted me to hear,
how much it meant to you.
And now I wish you knew
how often I turn to music,
how I'd love to say:
"So, who wrote this?"
sometimes needing to know,
sometimes just to show you:
Shostakovitch! Mahler!
Bartok! Brahms!

Wishing I'd Asked

You might have been walking into a sunset,
music swelling, credits rolling, the audience
of patients in the Day Centre reaching for handbags,

the way you insisted you could make the length of the room
alone, carrying your crossbar with its pouch of blood
and plasma like a banner, an eagle, towards what we knew

you were facing. But if anyone had asked
the Standard Bearer of the Ninth Legion what he saw
approaching, would he have answered? What would you have sai

At the Manor, Hemingford Grey

If they were lucky they came here
from the airfield. I picture summer
evenings too light for blackout,
fields billowing green and gold
under a sky as wide as it gets – carloads
of airmen between flights, between dog-fights,
legs stretched out awkwardly
from seats of stacked mattresses,
surrendering to the miraculous music
spooled out by this bamboo stylus –
Mozart's Clarinet Quintet
which I am listening to fifty years later
in the same room, remembering
your wartime stories – and that one
about how you drew aeroplanes all over
your 11+ paper, and how lucky you were
to be so bad at maths you couldn't become
a pilot, one of the one-in-four
who lost a lifetime of listening.

Replay

You went for words.
You'd arrange and rearrange
w, g, d, i, f, e, n, miss turns hoping
to swap 'w' for another 'e' to get
'feigned'. While I'd go for loose letters,
that 's' I could slip onto your 'blazer'
and make my 'exit' a triple.

It was guile playing clever.
You would often beat me
with words I'd never heard of,
like 'thole' and 'odal'. And I
got on your nerves by doing
the crossword on the side
while you were thinking.

So it should have been you
not me to achieve the 50+
double word starter score
with 'jackpot'. Luck not guile,
but I might have switched
the 'e' for 't' the way I feel
as if I'd cheated you out of it.

Knowing how to Live

We'd eaten the sweet onions
of the Cevennes, argued
over the implausibility
of vegetarianism to the French,

drunk all the other diners home.
We were leaving, they were closing,
but the Patronne was friendly
and our French getting perfect

when gusts of singing issued
from the unisex toilets. You
were playing the water-pedals
under each basin like an organ

and belting out 'The Lost Chord'
in your still hefty tenor. "Chic!"
exclaimed the Patronne, "Il est bon
viveur, le papa!" Oh, you were.

Unfrozen

When she can no longer put off sorting out
the shed, she comes across the tapes they'd emptied
from the Astra's side pockets when they sold it.

Elgar, Charlie Parker, Bach, and some unlabelled ones
she begins to check while washing up. One's a story.
Water cools as she listens, waiting for the end

but when it comes the tape continues – sounds
of someone in another room, crockery, a whirring,
a humming she can't place until she recognizes herself

in the kitchen years ago. And now she's sure
she's making ice cream. Probably rum-and-raisin
which never really froze. Or pistachio. At any moment

she'll add those extra drops of colouring to get the green
right, put it in the freezer. And he'll come in from work
or, better still, his studio where he'll have been

translating a painting into a linocut,
evening sunlight lengthening the garden beyond the window,
with her somewhere about the place. His idea of heaven.

Sky

All over the spare room floor
and still spreading,
grey-blue, blue-green,
palest of pinks, bleached
indigo – water colour
skies you painted –
your last twelve shirts,
worn to softness, unpicked
and pressed for patchwork.

I didn't know
they'd reach under everything –
bed, chairs, bookcase,
right out onto the landing –
or how long I would need
to keep rearranging the pieces
before I'd know where to begin.

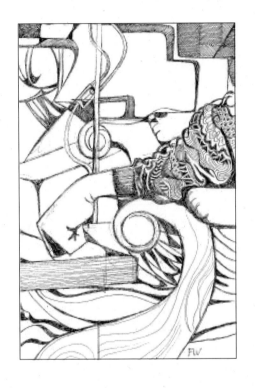